Classic Recipes of
SWEDEN

Classic Recipes of
SWEDEN

TRADITIONAL FOOD AND COOKING
IN 25 AUTHENTIC DISHES

ANNA MOSESSON

LORENZ BOOKS

This edition is published by Lorenz Books
info@anness.com

www.lorenzbooks.com
www.annesspublishing.com

If you like the images in this book
and would like to investigate using
them for publishing, promotions or
advertising, please visit our website
www.practicalpictures.com
for more information.

A CIP catalogue record for this book is
available from the British Library

Publisher: Joanna Lorenz
Editor: Emma Clegg & Helen Sudell
Designer: Nigel Partridge
Production: Ben Worley
Recipe Photography: William Lingwood

PUBLISHER'S NOTE

Although the advice and information in this
book are believed to be accurate and true
at the time of going to press, neither the
authors nor the publisher can accept any
legal responsibility or liability for any errors
or omissions that may have been made nor
for any inaccuracies nor for any loss, harm
or injury that comes about from following
instructions or advice in this book.

PUBLISHER'S ACKNOWLEDGMENTS

The Publisher would like to thank the
following agencies for the use of their
images. Alamy: p10tr; p11 both.
iStockphoto: p6, p13

COOK'S NOTES

Bracketed terms are intended for American
readers. For all recipes, quantities are
given in both metric and imperial measures
and, where appropriate, in standard cups
and spoons. Follow one set of measures,
but not a mixture, because they are
not interchangeable.

Standard spoon and cup measures are
level. 1 tsp = 5ml, 1 tbsp = 15ml, 1 cup =
250ml/8fl oz. Australian standard
tablespoons are 20ml. Australian readers
should use 3 tsp in place of 1 tbsp for
measuring small quantities.

American pints are 16fl oz/2 cups.
American readers should use 20fl oz/
2.5 cups in place of 1 pint when
measuring liquids.

Electric oven temperatures in this book are
for conventional ovens. When using a fan
oven, the temperature will probably need to
be reduced by about 10–20°C/20–40°F.
Since ovens vary, you should check
with your manufacturer's instruction
book for guidance.

The nutritional analysis given for each
recipe is calculated per portion (i.e. serving
or item), unless otherwise stated. If the
recipe gives a range, such as Serves 4–6,
then the nutritional analysis will be for the
smaller portion size, i.e. 6 servings. The
analysis does not include optional
ingredients, such as salt added to taste.

Medium (US large) eggs are used unless
otherwise stated.

Front cover shows Toast Skagen – for
recipe see page 21.

Contents

Introduction

Sweden nestles between Norway and Finland and over half the land is covered in forest and woodland. Wildlife such as elk (moose), reindeer (caribou), grouse and hare populate the forests, and these are also home to many species of mushroom and native berries. The long coastline, and a myriad of freshwater lakes ensure that there is a wide variety of fish to be eaten, culminating in a diet that is rich in flavour and intensity. No food experience can be topped by the use of such natural, fresh, seasonal produce and the Swedish take full advantage of this in their home cooking.

Left: Sheep and goats roam freely on the Isle of Gotland, northern Sweden. Cheese made from sheep's milk is very popular throughout Scandinavia.

Swedish Eating Traditions

Because of the extreme climate, the traditional Swedish approach to eating emphasized the need to preserve and store most of the fresh produce obtained in the warmer months to make it last throughout the year. Even eating fresh berries was a real treat, because berries were collected and made into jam to use in the winter. Swedish home cooking, or husmanskost, was born from the need for such preserved

Below: Open sandwiches of cheese, ham and salad are often eaten at breakfast.

Above: Raspberries are picked in late summer to make jam for the winter months.

food. Husmanskost consists of plain, rustic dishes and classics include meatballs, yellow pea soup, and stuffed cabbage rolls.

In more recent times the best of the traditional recipes have been modernized so that they are less hearty and simpler to prepare. Fresh fruit and vegetables have been added, traditional fatty dishes have been replaced with steaks, and stews and sauces have been made lighter.

Swedes eat three main meals. Breakfast usually consists of open sandwiches

with hard cheese or slices of meat. Yogurt and fermented milk are common and are served with cereals such as muesli, granola or porridge.

Lunch tends to be a light snack such as a sandwich whereas the evening meal is normally hot. At the table Swedes like to serve themselves and it is therefore considered polite to finish what one has served oneself.

The most well-known eating style in Sweden is the smörgåsbord, or bread-and-butter table. Dating from the 16th century, this was a tradition that saw all the food for a meal placed on the table at the same time. Originally the dishes were simple but as the custom continued, more and more dishes were added. Nowadays smörgåsbord is prepared for very special occasions such as Christmas, Easter and the festival of Midsummer.

Right: A traditional smörgåsbord will feature cured fish, eggs and pickled vegetables.

Swedish Food and Festivals

Feasts and festivals play an important part in the Swedish calendar. Many of them are closely associated with the changing seasons. Summer is celebrated with understandable intensity by a people who have endured a long, dark winter.

Our Lady's Day

On the 25th March farmers celebrate Vårfrudagen, or Our Lady's Day. Delicious waffles are made and eaten throughout the day. Toppings for the waffles vary and include fried salty bacon, or cloudberry jam and whipped cream.

Below: Waffles and fruit sauce are eaten on Our Lady's Day.

Easter

Swedish legend has it that on Maundy Thursday witches fly off on their broomsticks to a blue mountain where they would be entertained by the devil. Today children still dress up as witches and shout 'Glad Påsk' (Happy Easter) in return for treats. Halibut is often served on Good Friday, on the evening of Easter Saturday most Swedes will have a small smörgåsbord, and the Easter Sunday meal will be either roasted lamb or pork with hasselback potatoes.

Valborgsmässa

Soon after the Easter holiday, Valborgsmässa is celebrated on the 1st May to give thanks for the end of winter. The night before, huge bonfires made from juniper bushes are lit all over the country, and the smell creates a magical atmosphere.

Midsummer's Eve

This major festival takes place on the weekend nearest to 21st June. Traditionally everyone dances around a maypole, and

Above: A young Swedish girl dressed up as an Easter witch.

folk songs are sung. The drinking and eating continue for almost 24 hours as it hardly gets dark at this time of year.

Surströmming season

During this short season in August the tradition is to eat a strange and pungent dish. This Baltic herring dish from northern Sweden dates back to the 16th century. The herring is salted and fermented in a wooden barrel for six weeks and then canned. It is eaten with boiled potatoes, raw onion and bread. The smell when the can is opened is almost unbearable.

The Day of Santa Lucia

At the end of the year, the Swedes celebrate light, for the long dark winters can induce a feeling of melancholy over the community. The Day of Santa Lucia, the Queen of Light, falls on the 13th December.

A young girl (or several young girls) is chosen to represent the saint and processes through the village wearing a crown of candles in her hair, although today they are usually electric. After the procession, coffee is served with Lucia Saffron Buns and Gingerbread Biscuits.

Below: Christmas cookies are highly decorative.

Christmas

The Day of Santa Lucia marks the beginning of the magical Christmas season. The climax is Christmas Eve (Julafton), when smörgåsbord is served at lunchtime. A Christmas ham glazed with mustard and breadcrumbs is the centrepiece and other traditional Christmas dishes include Glassblower's herrings, pork sausage, potatoes and vört bread. The meal ends with coffee and Christmas cookies. In the evening, dishes include lutfisk, a speciality of both Sweden and

Above: A traditional Queen of Light festival on St Lucia's day.

Norway, which is a dish with a jelly-like consistency made from dried cod or ling soaked in a lye solution and then boiled. It is served with a white sauce, melted butter, peas, new potatoes and mustard. Dessert is typically julgröt, Sweden's traditional creamed rice pudding, which has a lucky almond hidden inside. Some Swedes make their julgröt more traditionally, using barley instead of rice.

Classic Ingredients

Cultivated landscapes in Sweden are home to a range of domestic animals and crops from chickens and pigs to potatoes and corn. Dairy farms are also common. The country's many deep forests and wetlands have a variety of wild animals and game, as well as the mushrooms and wild berries that feature largely in their diet. Sweden's plethora of lakes and long coastline provide a diversity of fish.

Wild and domestic animals

The hunting of hare, elk (moose), deer and reindeer (caribou) is a popular sport in

Below: Venison is an ideal meat to cure for the winter months.

Sweden. Venison is the name for deer meat, which can be roe deer, red deer, fallow deer or reindeer. Its flesh is dark red, lean and has a gamey flavour. Reindeer is a small deer and in Sweden it is eaten fresh, smoked and dried. It is also salted and cold-smoked to preserve it. The elk is a member of the deer family and eats only moss. The meat has very little fat, but a rich, fine flavour that differs from all other venison.

Pork is a staple food, and wild boar has recently been introduced as an animal for hunting enthusiasts, and it can now be found in Stockholm markets. Many delicious sausages are also produced.

Cows and sheep graze in meadows, resulting in a variety of dairy products, particularly cheese, and a regular supply of excellent lamb and beef.

Chickens are commonly kept, but while they are eaten, other birds, such as grouse, partridge or geese are preferred. Chickens are mainly valued in Sweden for their eggs.

Above: Baltic herring is only found in the Baltic sea.

Fish and seafood

Saltwater fishing from the west coast provides cod, haddock, and salmon, while Baltic herring, pike, perch and zaner are plentiful in the Stockholm archipelago. Freshwater crayfish are caught in the lakes and rivers. Swedish fish and shellfish have a reputation for their rich flavours and fine consistency, a result of natural, slow growth in cold, clear waters. Fish roe is used widely in Swedish cuisine, especially trout and salmon roe.

Right: Reindeer live mainly in the Northern forests of Sweden and are considered a delicacy.

Above: The humble potato is loved by all Swedes.

Crops

The more fertile soil in the south favours arable farming. This is where the potato, universally loved by the local population, is grown, along with other vegetable crops such as beetroot (beet), cabbage, kale, carrots, corn, leeks, broccoli, cucumber and peas. Barley, wheat, rye and oats are also grown, as well as oilseed rape and sugar beet.

The Swedes are very conscientious about their health and have strict regulations on how crops are grown, for how long, and what fertilizers are used. In the winter months Swedish soil is allowed to rest and recover, in many areas under a protective covering of snow.

Dairy

Many dairy products play a role in Swedish cuisine. Milk, cream and butter form the basis of delicious desserts, and creamy pastries and cheese are eaten in large quantities.

The country boasts almost 200 different cheeses, most of which are semi-soft, and these are made from cow's, sheep's or goat's milk. For breakfast the Swedes usually eat a soft cheese such as Kvark.

Below: There are many types of semi-soft cheese in Sweden.

Västerbotten, sometimes called "Swedish Parmesan", is a semi-hard cheese similar in flavour to a very strong English Cheddar or Italian Reggiano Parmesan, and is considered by many to be the best Swedish cheese. The semi-soft cheeses include Grevé, which resembles Swiss Emmenthal with a sweet mild flavour. A popular blue cheese is Adelost and an excellent blue cheese, made from sheep's milk in southern Gotland, is Wanås.

Mushrooms

Wild mushrooms are plentiful in Sweden and locals have a passion for gathering and eating them. Good places to find mushrooms are jealously guarded secrets among both serious collectors and casual harvesters of these earthy fruits of the forest.

In Sweden, the most highly regarded mushroom is the chanterelle, which is usually served with a piece of meat, or simply fried with a cream sauce and some onions and served in

Above: The porcini, or cep, mushroom adds earthy flavour.

a sandwich. Sweden also has a reputation for good porcini mushrooms. Famous for their flavour and earthy smell, many tonnes are exported each year.

Wild berries and fruits

Berries are widely available throughout Sweden and, when in season, you will find many people in the woods gathering them. Varieties include wild cloudberries, lingonberries bilberries, and buckthorn, as well as strawberries, blackberries and raspberries. They are all very high in vitamin C, especially lingonberries. Cloudberries, amber-coloured raspberry-sized berries, are the rarest variety and only come from the north of Sweden. Lingonberries, however, tiny, tart red berries that belong to the cranberry family, can be found all over Sweden and are exported abroad. Most lingonberries are preserved as a sauce or jam, when they are simply stirred with sugar and then put straight into jars – their citric acid content is so high that they need no cooking. They are delicious served with wild meats such as elk (moose) and roe deer, but frequently the lingonberry preserve is served with hotly spiced meatballs.

Below: Cloudberries are picked in the wild every autumn.

Above: Lingonberries are rich in Vitamin C.

Bilberries, or blåbär as the Swedish call them, grow in the same woodland areas as lingonberries. They are like a small version of the cultivated blueberry and are good for making into jam or using in sweet pies. The Swedes also make a bilberry soup and a rosehip soup, both of which are popular desserts but are frequently eaten at breakfast time with yogurt.

Other berries such as raspberries, blueberries and strawberries are traditionally used to make a delectable fruit compote called drottningkräm, again often served at breakfast.

Land of the Northern Lights

Traditional Swedish cooking is hearty and based around fish from Sweden's extensive coastline and lakes, rich game meat such as venison and reindeer, forest mushrooms and wild berries harvested from the hedgerows. Its popularity today is a testament to the values of using fresh local ingredients cooked simply to retain maximum taste. From Elk Meatballs with Lingon and Reindeer Stroganoff to Cloudberry Soufflé and Waffles with Spiced Blueberry Compote, the selection of authentic recipes that follow clearly illustrate this tradition.

Left: Freshly picked berries, rich in vitamin C, feature in many Swedish desserts.

Yellow Pea Soup
Ärtsoppa

Serves 6–8

500g/1¼lb yellow split peas
30ml/2 tbsp vegetable oil
1 Spanish (Bermuda) onion, sliced
500g/1¼lb salted pork belly or
    bacon
2 litres/3½ pints/8 cups water or
    ham stock
bay leaf
1 bunch thyme sprigs
5ml/1 tsp chopped fresh thyme
    and/or marjoram
Swedish mustard and rye bread,
    to serve

1 Soak the yellow split peas in cold water overnight. The next day, drain them and put to one side.

2 Heat the oil in a large, heavy pan, add the onion and pork belly and when browned, add the water or ham stock. Heat until simmering then skim off any foam and cook for about 1 hour.

3 Add the peas, bay leaf and thyme sprigs and leave to cook for a further hour until the peas are soft and the pork is completely cooked and falling apart.

4 Remove the pork from the pan and cut it into cubes, then return it to the pan with the fresh thyme and/or marjoram.

5 Season the soup with salt to taste before serving, although because the meat is salty, the soup may not need extra seasoning. Serve the soup with Swedish mustard and a hard bread such as rye bread.

In the Middle Ages, this nourishing soup was always served on Thursdays to prepare the population for the Christian weekend fast that started on Friday.

Nettle Soup with Egg Butterballs
Näselsoppa med ägg

Serves 6–8

a knob (pat) of butter

1 onion, roughly chopped

225g/8oz nettles (top 4 leaves from each plant only) or young spinach leaves

600ml/1 pint/2½ cups chicken stock

30ml/2 tbsp sherry

150ml/¼ pint/⅔ cup double (heavy) cream

5ml/½ tsp freshly grated nutmeg

salt and ground black pepper

For the butterballs

115g/4oz/½ cup butter

2 hard-boiled egg yolks

salt and ground black pepper

Nettle soup is extremely nutritious but as nettles cannot be found all year around, as an alternative you can use spinach, which goes equally well with the butterballs.

1 First make the butterballs. Put the butter and hard-boiled egg yolks in a bowl and mash together. Season the mixture with salt and pepper to taste. Roll into balls approximately 2cm/1in in diameter and chill in the refrigerator until ready to serve.

2 To make the soup, melt the butter in a saucepan, add the onion and fry until softened. Add the nettles or spinach, stir in the stock and season with salt and pepper. Bring to the boil then cook over a medium heat for 1 minute.

3 Pour the soup into a food processor and whiz until roughly chopped. Return to the pan, add the sherry, stir in the cream and sprinkle with nutmeg. Heat gently until warm but do not allow the soup to boil. Serve in warmed bowls with the butterballs bobbing on the surface and just beginning to melt.

Lacy Potato Pancakes Råraka

Serves 6

6 large potatoes
1 leek, finely sliced
1 carrot, grated (optional)
15g/½oz butter
15ml/1 tbsp vegetable oil
salt and ground black pepper

For the topping

12 slices of smoked salmon
250ml/8fl oz/1 cup sour cream
1 red onion, finely diced

These pretty, lacy pancakes should be served as an accompaniment to a fish dish or smoked salmon. In Sweden, small ones are often served as canapés at parties.

1 Peel and grate the potatoes. Put in a bowl, add the leek and carrot, if using, and mix them all together.

2 Heat the butter and oil in a frying pan and when smoking, add spoonfuls of the potato mixture to make 7.5cm/3in pancakes. Fry the pancakes, turning once, until golden brown on both sides. Season with salt and pepper.

3 Serve hot topped with slices of smoked salmon, sour cream and diced red onion.

Toast Skagen Skagenröra

Serves 6–8

1kg/2¼lb shell-on cooked prawns (shrimp)
250ml/8fl oz/1 cup sour cream
250ml/8fl oz/1 cup thick mayonnaise
30ml/2 tbsp chopped fresh dill plus fronds, to garnish
30ml/2 tbsp chopped fresh chives
a squeeze of lemon juice
25–50g/1–2oz/2–4 tbsp butter
8 slices bread, halved
5ml/1 tsp red lumpfish roe
salt and ground black pepper

1 Carefully remove the shells from the prawns, keeping them intact. Put the sour cream, mayonnaise, chopped dill, chives and lemon juice in a large bowl. Season with salt and pepper to taste then stir in the prawns.

2 Melt the butter in a large frying pan, add the bread slices and fry until golden brown on both sides.

3 Serve the prawn mixture piled on top of the fried bread and garnish with a small amount of the lumpfish roe and a frond of dill.

COOK'S TIP
Salmon roe is ideal to use as a garnish, as its beautiful orange colour and large eggs makes the dish look rather special. Grated horseradish is another good accompaniment.

This dish originates from the west coast of Sweden, between Sweden and Denmark. Skagenröra, which translates as "a mixture from the sea", is often served in restaurants as a tasty seafood snack. You can use peeled prawns, but those with their shell on taste and look better.

Serves 6–8

1kg/2¼lb fresh salmon, filleted and
    boned, with skin on
50g/2oz/½ cup sea salt
50g/2oz/½ cup caster (superfine)
    sugar
10ml/2 tsp crushed white
    peppercorns
200g/7oz/2 cups chopped fresh dill
    with stalks
fresh dill fronds, to garnish

For the mustard and dill sauce

100g/4oz Swedish mustard
100g/4oz/½ cup caster (superfine)
    sugar
15ml/1 tbsp vinegar
5ml/1 tsp salt
ground black pepper
300ml/½ pint/1¼ cups vegetable oil
100g/4oz/2 cups chopped fresh
    dill fronds

Gravlax with Mustard and Dill Sauce Gravlax med gravlax sås

1 Using tweezers, remove any pinbones from the salmon. Then mix the salt and sugar together. Sprinkle a little of the mixture on a sheet of foil and place half the salmon fillet, skin side down, on the mixture. Sprinkle the salmon with a little more of the salt and sugar mixture.

2 Sprinkle the white pepper on the flesh side of both salmon fillets and then add the chopped dill to both fillets. Place the second salmon fillet, skin side up, on top of the first fillet and finally sprinkle over the remaining salt and sugar mixture.

3 Wrap the foil around the salmon fillets and leave in the refrigerator for 48 hours, turning the salmon every 12 hours. (The foil contains all the juices which help to marinate the salmon.)

4 To make the sauce, put the mustard, sugar, vinegar and salt and pepper into a bowl and mix them all together. Then very slowly drizzle the oil into the mixture, whisking it all the time until you end up with a thick, shiny sauce. Finally add the chopped dill to the mixture.

5 When the salmon has marinated slice it thinly, from one end, at an angle of 45 degrees. Either serve the gravlax on individual serving plates or on one large dish with the dill and mustard sauce on the side. Garnish with dill fronds.

Home-made gravlax has no comparison. The name, with "grav" meaning hole in the ground and "lax" meaning salmon, derives from the fact that it used to be prepared by burying it underground to cure, so that it would remain cool. The key to successful gravlax is the mustard and dill sauce with which it is served.

Stuffed Cabbage Rolls Kåldomar

Serves 6–8

1 Savoy cabbage
100g/4oz/½ cup long grain rice
100ml/4fl oz/½ cup water
15g/½oz/1 tbsp butter
1 large Spanish (Bermuda) onion,
    chopped
250g/9oz minced (ground) beef
1 egg, beaten
2.5ml/½ tsp chopped fresh thyme
5ml/1 tsp salt
ground black pepper
melted butter for brushing
boiled new potatoes and lingonberry
    conserve, to serve

1 Cut the base off the cabbage and separate the leaves. Cook in boiling salted water for 1 minute, drain and remove the hard centre of each cabbage leaf.

2 Put the rice and water in a pan, bring to the boil then simmer for 10–12 minutes until the rice is tender. Drain and leave to cool.

3 Preheat the oven to 200°C/400°F/Gas 6. Melt the butter in a pan, add the onion and fry until softened. Put the minced beef in a large bowl and add the onion, cooled rice, beaten egg, thyme, salt and pepper to season.

4 Put 30ml/2 tbsp of the mixture into each leaf and wrap into parcels. Brush the parcels with melted butter and place in an ovenproof dish.

5 Bake for about 40 minutes until golden brown. Serve with boiled new potatoes and lingonberry conserve.

After Karl XII's invasion of Turkey in 1713 his soldiers brought this dish back to Sweden and replaced the vine leaves with cabbage leaves. Kåldomar are often served as part of the Christmas table in Sweden with a brown sauce.

Jansson's Temptation
Jansson's frestelse

1 Preheat the oven to 180°C/350°F/Gas 4. Peel and grate the potatoes. Put in a sieve (strainer) and wash under cold running water to remove any excess starch. Drain well and put in a bowl. Add the sliced onion and mix together then put in a shallow, ovenproof dish.

2 Mix together the milk and cream. Put both the liquid and the fish from the can of anchovies into the milk mixture and stir together. Pour the mixture over the potatoes and season with salt and pepper. Bake in the oven for 50 minutes until golden brown and bubbling.

COOK'S TIPS
• This dish is delicious served on its own or with a salad and is also perfect when eaten with cold sliced ham.
• If you cannot get Swedish anchovies, use ordinary salted anchovies and soak them in milk for a couple of hours to remove the saltiness.

Serves 6
6 large potatoes
1 Spanish (Bermuda) onion, thinly
    sliced
120ml/4fl oz/½ cup milk
250ml/8fl oz/1 cup double (heavy)
    cream
100g/3½oz can Swedish anchovies
salt and ground black pepper

This anchovy pie is another warming dish for the winter months. The dish is named after a well-known Swedish opera singer who served it to his guests after a performance at the opera house in Stockholm. In Sweden, a meal such as this, called "vickning", is served late in the evening at the end of a good party, and is always accompanied by schnapps. It is also excellent served as part of a smörgåsbord selection.

Poached Turbot with Egg and Prawns
Kokt piggvar med ägg, räk och pepparot sås

Serves 6–8

1kg/2¼lb whole turbot, gutted
1 leek, finely chopped
1 bunch fresh parsley, chopped
1 lemon, sliced
salt and ground black pepper

For the sauce

1 egg
250g/9oz/1 cup plus 2 tbsp butter
175g/6oz shell-on cooked prawns
    (shrimp)
15ml/1 tbsp grated fresh horseradish

1 Preheat the oven to 180°C/350°F/Gas 4. Lay the gutted turbot on a large sheet of foil.

2 Mix together the chopped leek and parsley and season with salt and pepper.

3 Use the leek and parsley mixture to stuff the body cavity of the turbot and then add the lemon slices. Wrap the turbot in the foil and bake the fish in the oven for 45 minutes.

4 To make the sauce, hard boil the egg and leave to cool. Then mash the hard-boiled egg in a bowl.

5 Melt the butter and set aside. Remove the shells from the prawns and add them to the mashed hard-boiled egg with the butter and grated horseradish.

6 Serve the turbot on a large serving dish, accompanied by the sauce.

COOK'S TIPS
• Ask your fishmonger to gut the turbot.
• Turbot is a flat fish and it is advisable to prepare it when it is a couple of days old so that the meat becomes firmer and develops more flavour.

Turbot, known as the king of flat fish because of its firm, white flesh and delicate flavour, is found mostly in the North Sea on the west coast of Sweden. In Sweden, turbot is often irreverently called "dass lock", meaning toilet seat, which is a reference to its expansive flat shape. If unavailable, halibut, sole or flounder are good substitutes.

Fried Mackerel with Rhubarb Chutney
Makril med rabarber chutney

Serves 6

6 mackerel fillets, skinned
60ml/4 tbsp plain (all-purpose) white
   flour
30ml/2 tbsp vegetable oil
25g/1oz/2 tbsp butter
salt and ground black pepper
boiled new potatoes, to serve

For the rhubarb chutney

150g/5oz fresh rhubarb
50g/2oz/¼ cup caster (superfine)
   sugar
5ml/1 tsp cider vinegar
a knob (pat) of butter

*Mackerel is an undervalued
and inexpensive fish. It has
a wonderful flavour and, as
an oily fish, is very good for
you. Because of its oiliness
and distinctive flavour it is
best served with something
a little tart such as a
squeeze of lemon or, as in
this recipe, rhubarb.*

1 To make the rhubarb chutney, cut the rhubarb into small pieces and put in a pan with the sugar and vinegar. Simmer for about 6 minutes until soft but not mushy. Stir in the butter.

2 Dust the mackerel with the flour and season with salt and pepper. Heat the oil and butter in a large frying pan, add the mackerel fillets and fry for 2–3 minutes on each side until golden brown.

3 Warm the chutney in the pan. Serve the mackerel with the rhubarb chutney and new potatoes.

COOK'S TIP
Replace the rhubarb in the chutney recipe with gooseberries to make gooseberry chutney instead.

Lax Pudding
Lax pudding

Serves 8
250g/9oz new potatoes
25g/1oz/2 tbsp butter
1 leek, sliced
200g/7oz gravlax, about 8 slices
a little chopped fresh dill
2 eggs
250ml/8fl oz/1 cup milk
30ml/2 tbsp double (heavy) cream
salt and ground black pepper

This mouthwatering winter warmer – a classic dish from the Swedish husmanskost, or home cooking – is an excellent way to use up any remaining smoked salmon or gravlax. This is a good alternative to fish pie, with similar ingredients, but a quite different preparation method. The dill is what makes Lax Pudding so essentially Swedish.

1 Cook the potatoes in boiling salted water for 15–20 minutes until tender. Drain and leave to cool. Meanwhile, melt the butter in a pan. Add the sliced leek and sauté gently until softened.

2 Preheat the oven to 180°C/350°F/Gas 4. Thinly slice the cooled potatoes and place in a layer in the bottom of a terrine. Add 1–3 slices of gravlax and then add a layer of leeks. Repeat these layers, using all the ingredients, and finishing with a neat layer of potatoes. Sprinkle over the chopped dill.

3 Beat the eggs in a large bowl. Add the milk and cream and beat together then season with salt and pepper.

4 Pour the egg mixture into the terrine. Bake in the oven for about 30 minutes until golden brown on top.

Salted Salmon with Potatoes in Dill Sauce
Rimmad lax med dillstuvad potatis

Serves 6–8

200g/7oz/2 cups sea salt
50g/2oz/½ cup caster (superfine)
    sugar
1kg/2¼lb salmon, scaled, filleted
    and boned
1 litre/1¾ pints/4 cups water
675–900g/1½–2lb new potatoes

For the béchamel and dill sauce

25g/1oz/2 tbsp butter
45ml/3 tbsp plain (all-purpose) flour
750ml/1¼ pints/3 cups milk
120ml/4fl oz/½ cup double (heavy)
    cream
a little freshly grated nutmeg
    (optional)
25g/1oz/¼ cup chopped fresh dill
salt and ground black pepper

1 Mix together 100g/4oz/1 cup of the salt and the sugar. Cover the salmon fillets with the mixture and put in a plastic bag. Seal the bag and put the fish on a plate in the refrigerator overnight.

2 The next day, make a brine by mixing the remaining salt and the water in a bowl. Place the salmon in the brine and leave in the refrigerator for another night.

3 Remove the salmon from the brine and cut into 5mm/¼in slices. If large, cut the potatoes in half then cook in boiling water for about 20 minutes until tender.

4 Meanwhile, make the béchamel sauce. Melt the butter in a pan, add the flour and cook over a low heat for 1 minute, stirring to make a roux. Remove from the heat and slowly add the milk, stirring all the time, to form a smooth sauce. Return to the heat and cook, stirring, for 2–3 minutes until the sauce boils and thickens. Stir in the cream, nutmeg if using, salt and pepper to taste and heat gently.

5 Drain the cooked potatoes and add to the sauce with the chopped dill. Serve the salted salmon with the potatoes in béchamel and dill.

Rimmad lax or salted salmon is a refreshing alternative to the more commonly known gravlax recipe. Personally, I prefer rimmad lax, because it is plumper, smoother and fresher. This dish is delicious with creamy potatoes and dill, which counteracts the saltiness of the fish. Plan ahead for this dish as the salmon must marinate for 48 hours.

Stuffed Guinea Fowl with Wild Mushrooms
Pärlhöna med blandad svamp

1 Cook the pearl barley in a pan of lightly salted water for 1–2 hours until tender. Melt 25g/1oz/2 tbsp of the butter in a pan, add the mushrooms and sauté until the juices have evaporated. Add the parsley and soy sauce and leave to cool.

2 Skin the guinea fowl portions and put between 2 sheets of clear film (plastic wrap) and bash until flattened with a wooden rolling pin. Spread the cold mushroom stuffing on to the guinea fowl portions then roll them up carefully. Wrap each individually in clear film.

3 Preheat the oven to 180°C/350°F/Gas 4. Cut the vegetables into strips or cubes and put in an oiled roasting pan. Drizzle with the olive oil, season and roast in the oven for approximately 20 minutes until tender.

4 Thirty minutes before the barley is cooked, put the wrapped breasts in a pan in a single layer and pour over the stock. Bring to the boil and simmer gently for 30 minutes.

5 Ten minutes before the barley is cooked, prepare the pearl barley risotto. Heat the oil in a pan, add the mushrooms and sauté.

6 Remove the cooked breasts from the stock and keep warm. Pour the stock into a jug (pitcher).

7 Melt the remaining butter, add the flour, and cook, stirring over a low heat for 1 minute to make a roux. Remove from the heat and add enough of the reserved stock to form a gravy. Return to the heat and stir for 2–3 minutes until the gravy thickens. Season to taste.

8 Drain the pearl barley and add to the mushrooms with the garlic and parsley. Stir together. Unwrap the breasts, slice carefully and place on warmed serving plates. Serve with the gravy, roasted vegetables and pearl barley risotto.

Serves 8

25g/1oz/2 tbsp butter, plus
   15g/½oz/1 tbsp for the gravy
250g/9oz wild mushrooms, chopped
30ml/2 tbsp chopped fresh parsley
5ml/1 tsp soy sauce
8 guinea fowl breast portions
about 750ml/1¼ pints/3 cups
   chicken stock
15ml/1 tbsp plain (all-purpose) flour
salt and ground black pepper

For the pearl barley risotto

200g/7oz pearl barley
15ml/1 tbsp olive oil
100g/4oz mixed wild mushrooms
2 garlic cloves, crushed
100g/4oz fresh parsley, chopped

For the roasted vegetables

200g/7oz parsnips and carrots
120ml/4fl oz/½ cup olive oil

*Guinea fowl meat is white
like chicken but tastes
more like pheasant,
although with a less
gamey flavour.*

Gotland Lamb Burgers Stuffed with Blue Cheese Lamburgare från Gotland med ädelost

Serves 8

2 potatoes
60ml/4fl oz/½ cup milk
50g/2oz/4 tbsp butter
1 egg, beaten
1 red onion, chopped
100ml/4fl oz/½ cup crème fraîche
15ml/1 tbsp mustard seeds
400g/14oz minced (ground) lamb
225g/8oz/1 cup blue cheese, such
    as Gorgonzola or Stilton
salt and ground black pepper

1 Peel the potatoes, cut into quarters and cook in boiling water for about 20 minutes until tender. When the potatoes are cooked, drain, return to the pan and mash well. Heat the milk with 25g/1oz/2 tbsp of the butter and beat them well into the potato mash.

2 Put the mashed potatoes in a large bowl. Add the egg, chopped onion, crème fraîche, mustard seeds, salt and pepper and mix well together. Add the minced lamb and mix again.

3 Form the mixture into 16 even-size, round, flat burgers. Spoon a little of the blue cheese on the centre of 8 of the burgers and then place the remaining burgers on top to make 8 larger burgers.

4 Melt the remaining butter in a large frying pan. Add the burgers and fry for 3 minutes on each side, until golden brown and the cheese has melted. Serve hot.

COOK'S TIPS
The burgers can be made with minced (ground) venison. They are also good served with mashed potatoes and leeks sliced and lightly fried in butter.

Originating from the island of Gotland, the lamb adds a gamey, rich quality to these burgers, and the blue cheese and crème fraîche give them a creamy consistency. Lamb burgers are much healthier than beef burgers because they contain far less saturated fat.

Sailor's Steak Sjöman's biff

1 Preheat the oven to 180°C/350°F/Gas 4. Using a rolling pin or heavy wooden mallet, beat the steaks until flattened. Peel the potatoes, cut in half and then into 1cm/½in slices.

2 Melt the butter in a large flameproof casserole. Add the onions and fry for about 10 minutes until golden brown. Push the onions to one side of the dish, add the steaks and fry until sealed on both sides. Add the sliced potatoes, thyme, bay leaves, salt and pepper.

3 Pour the ale over the ingredients in the dish, cover with a lid and bake in the oven for about 1 hour until the potatoes are tender. Sprinkle chopped parsley on top to garnish and serve with pickled beetroot or pickled gherkins.

Serves 8

8 thin slices entrecôte (sirloin) steak,
    about 600g/1lb 6oz
8 medium potatoes
15g/½oz/1 tbsp butter
4 onions, chopped
1 sprig fresh thyme
2 bay leaves
500ml/17fl oz bottle ale
salt and ground black pepper
15ml/1 tbsp chopped fresh parsley,
    to garnish
pickled beetroot (beet) or pickled
    gherkins, to serve

Also known as seaman's beef, this dish used to be associated with sailors because it requires very few kitchen utensils and just one pot to make it. Cooking the meat and vegetables together gives the dish a delicious stew-like combination of textures and flavours.

Prune-stuffed Loin of Pork with Hasselback Potatoes Rostad fläsk stek med plommon

Serves 6–8

200g/7oz Agen prunes
15g/½oz/1 tbsp butter
1 Spanish (Bermuda) onion, chopped
15ml/1 tbsp chopped fresh parsley
500g/1¼lb boned loin of pork, with rind on
salt and ground black pepper

For the hasselback potatoes

1.3–1.8kg/3–4lb small roasting potatoes
100g/4oz/½ cup butter, melted
30ml/2 tbsp fresh breadcrumbs

The Swedes love the taste of pork and this recipe is a real favourite. Here, the roast pork is served with hasselback potatoes, which are the Swedish version of roast potatoes. They have a wonderful crispy crust and are delightfully easy to prepare.

1 Soak the prunes in cold water overnight. The next day, chop the prunes into small pieces. Melt the butter in a frying pan, add the onion and fry for about 5 minutes until beginning to soften. Add the chopped prunes and parsley and fry, stirring occasionally, until the onions are very soft and the mixture is slightly sticky. Season the mixture with salt and pepper to taste. Leave to cool while preparing the hasselback potatoes.

2 Preheat the oven to 220ºC/425ºF/Gas 7. Peel the potatoes so that they are evenly sized and oval. Put the potatoes, one at a time, on a wooden spoon and slice across their width at 5mm/¼in intervals, through the potato until you hit the wooden spoon. This stops you slicing all the way through. Then put the potatoes in a roasting pan and pour over the melted butter. Roast in the top of the oven for 10 minutes.

3 Meanwhile, open out the pork and place, skin side down, on a chopping board. Spread the prune stuffing over the pork, roll up and tie at regular intervals with string. Using a sharp knife score the skin then sprinkle with salt.

4 When the potatoes have roasted for 10 minutes, baste with the butter. Reduce the oven temperature to 180ºC/350ºF/Gas 4 and roast the pork in the oven, below the potatoes, for 40 minutes.

5 When the pork has roasted for 40 minutes, remove the potatoes from the oven, baste and sprinkle over the breadcrumbs. Return to the oven and roast the potatoes and pork for a further 20 minutes.

6 Remove the cooked pork from the oven and leave it to stand for 15 minutes. Meanwhile increase the oven temperature to 220ºC/425ºF/Gas 7 and roast the potatoes for a further 15 minutes until just golden brown and opened up like a fan. To serve, remove the crackling from the pork and carve the meat. Accompany with the hasselback potatoes.

Swedish Hash Pytt-i-panna

1 Peel and cut the potatoes into small cubes measuring about 3mm/⅛in. Heat the butter and oil in a large frying pan, add the potato cubes and fry for about 20 minutes, stirring frequently, until golden brown. Remove from the pan with a slotted spoon, put in a bowl and keep warm.

2 Put the onion in the pan, adding more butter if necessary, and fry until golden brown. Remove from the pan and add to the potatoes. Add the gammon or bacon and the frankfurter sausages, fry until cooked and put them in the bowl.

3 Fry the beef or lamb until heated through and add to the other fried ingredients. Season the mixture with salt and pepper to taste and mix together well.

4 Serve the mixture on warmed, individual serving plates. Break the eggs, one at a time, separating the yolks from the whites, and putting an egg yolk in half its shell in the centre of each plate. Garnish with chopped parsley and serve with Worcestershire sauce.

COOK'S TIPS
• 1–2 tablespoons of capers can be included in the mixture. Add them to the pan with the meat.
• Make sure that the eggs are fresh and, because the recipe contains raw egg yolks, do not serve the dish to infants, the elderly, pregnant women, or convalescents.
• The dish can also be served with fried eggs and beetroot (beet) or sour pickled gherkin.

A classic Swedish dish, "Pytt-i-panna" literally means put in the pan. Originally introduced as an economy dish made with leftovers, its popularity has meant that it is invariably now made from fresh ingredients.

Serves 3–4

4 large potatoes
about 25g/1oz/2 tbsp butter
15ml/1 tbsp vegetable oil
1 large onion, finely chopped
150g/5oz gammon (smoked or cured ham) or bacon, finely chopped
100g/4oz smoked frankfurters, finely chopped
500g/1¼lb cold cooked lamb or beef, cubed
salt and ground black pepper
3–4 very fresh eggs, to serve
Worcestershire sauce, to serve
chopped fresh parsley, to garnish

Baked Sausage Terrine with Lingonberry Conserve Korv terrine med lingon

Serves 6–8

115g/4oz/1 cup oatmeal
750ml/1¼ pints/3 cups water
750ml/1¼ pints/3 cups milk
15g/½oz/1 tbsp butter
1 red onion, finely chopped
200g/7oz pig's liver, minced (ground)
200g/7oz minced (ground) pork
150g/5oz/1 cup raisins
5ml/1 tsp chopped fresh marjoram
5ml/1 tsp ground allspice
salt and ground black pepper
lingonberry conserve and toast,
    to serve

This dish can be made with ready-made sausage meat (bulk sausage), or if you prefer you can make your own, as shown here, using a mixture of oatmeal, pig's liver, pork and raisins. The oatmeal gives a texture just like the sausage meat. The sweet lingonberry conserve is a perfect accompaniment.

1 Preheat the oven to 180°C/350°F/Gas 4. Line the base and sides of a 20cm/8in loaf tin (pan) with baking parchment.

2 Put the oatmeal, water and milk in a large pan, bring to the boil then reduce the heat and cook for 3–4 minutes until soft. Leave to cool.

3 Melt the butter in a pan, add the finely chopped onion and fry for 5–10 minutes until the onion is softened. Transfer the onion to a large bowl, add the cooled oatmeal, pig's liver, minced pork, raisins, marjoram, allspice, salt and pepper and mix well together.

4 Pour the mixture into the prepared tin, level the top and bake in the oven for 40 minutes–1 hour until lightly browned. Serve the sausage terrine hot or cold with lingonberry conserve and toast.

Reindeer Stroganoff
Ren stroganoff

Serves 6–8

1kg/2¼lb reindeer, roe deer or beef
    fillet
15g/½oz/1 tbsp butter
15ml/1 tbsp vegetable oil
2 Spanish (Bermuda) onions,
    chopped
8 juniper berries, crushed
15ml/1 tbsp plain (all-purpose) flour
45ml/3 tbsp tomato purée (paste)
45ml/3 tbsp Dijon mustard
475ml/16fl oz/2 cups double (heavy)
    cream
chopped fresh parsley, to garnish
boiled rice or pearl barley, to serve

The fillet used in this dish is the best cut of reindeer. The bitter gin flavour of the juniper berries is a strong complement to the wild meat. Beef is an excellent substitute meat or, for a more authentic taste, use roe deer which is similar to reindeer.

1 Cut the meat into 5mm/¼in x 5cm/2in strips. Heat the butter and oil in a large flameproof casserole, add the meat and fry for about 5 minutes until golden brown on all sides. Add the onions and juniper berries.

2 Stir the flour into the pan then, over a low heat, add the tomato purée, mustard and finally the cream and stir together. Simmer for about half an hour until the meat is tender. Garnish the dish with chopped parsley and serve with boiled rice or pearl barley.

COOK'S TIP

Garnishing the stroganoff with chopped parsley gives the dish more colour and freshness.

Elk Meatballs with Lingon
Alg Köttbullar med lingon

The meatballs serve 12–14;
the sauce serves 6

1 large potato
100g/4oz/½ cup butter
1kg/2¼lb red onions, finely chopped
150g/5oz/2½ cups fresh
    breadcrumbs
300ml/½ pint/1¼ cups double
    (heavy) cream
105ml/7 tbsp full-fat (whole) milk
5ml/1 tsp sugar
ground white pepper
10ml/2 tsp salt
3kg/6¾lb minced (ground) elk
    (moose) or 1kg/2¼lb best quality
    minced (ground) pork and
    2kg/4½lb best quality minced
    (ground) steak
6 eggs, beaten
handful of chopped fresh parsley
about 45ml/3 tbsp vegetable oil
mashed potatoes and lingonberry
    conserve, to serve

For the cream sauce
120ml/4fl oz/½ cup Amontillado
    sherry
250ml/8fl oz/1 cup double (heavy)
    cream
30ml/2 tbsp soy sauce (optional)

1 Cut the potato into quarters and cook in boiling water for 15–20 minutes until tender, then drain and mash. Melt 75g/3oz/16 tbsp of the butter in a frying pan, add the onions and fry until softened.

2 Put the mashed potato, onions, breadcrumbs, cream and milk in a large bowl and mix together. Leave to swell for a few minutes then add the sugar, season generously with pepper and add the salt. Add the elk or pork and steak mince, the eggs and parsley and mix thoroughly together. Leave to stand for 1 hour to allow the flavours to infuse.

3 Roll the mixture into meatballs that are about the size of a small apricot. (At this stage, if it is more convenient you can freeze half the quantity of meatballs to use on another occasion.)

4 Heat the remaining butter and the oil in a large frying pan, add the meatballs and fry in batches to avoid over-crowding the pan, for about 10 minutes until browned. (You may need to add a little more oil to the pan but this will depend on how much fat there is in the meat.) Using a slotted spoon, remove the meatballs from the pan, transfer to a warmed serving dish and keep warm.

5 To make the cream sauce, add the sherry to the pan and stir to deglaze the pan. Stir in the cream, add the soy sauce if using, and heat gently. Pour the sauce over the meatballs and serve hot, with mashed potatoes and lingonberry conserve.

Meatballs are probably the best-known Swedish dish and are especially delicious when home-made. Always make a large quantity to make the most of your time because they do take a while to prepare.

Carpaccio of Cured Venison
Tunt skivat gravad hjort

1 Remove all stringy parts from the venison fillet then place on a sheet of foil. Mix the salt and sugar together and sprinkle the mixture over the fillet. Add the thyme leaves and season with pepper.

2 Wrap the fillet in the foil and leave in the refrigerator to cure for 48 hours, turning every 12 hours. Transfer the fillet to the freezer and store for up to 1 week before serving.

3 Thinly slice the meat while it is still frozen, when it is much easier to slice. Thaw the fillet for a minimum of 10 hours in the refrigerator. Just before serving, place the sliced meat on serving plates and drizzle with a little olive oil and lemon juice. Serve with a crisp green salad and Melba toast.

Serves 6–8

1kg/2¼lb venison fillet
50g/2oz/½ cup sea salt
50g/2oz/¼ cup caster (superfine) sugar
1 bunch fresh thyme, leaves stripped
5ml/1 tsp ground black pepper
olive oil and lemon juice, for drizzling
crisp green salad and Melba toast, to serve

Carpaccio of venison is a modern cured-meat dish. It is a good alternative to gravlax and is prepared in a similar way, the only difference being that fresh thyme flavours the meat instead of dill. You can use elk, reindeer or any other venison for this dish. Because it needs to be made in advance and frozen, the dish requires only a little preparation on the day.

Glögg Jelly with Clove Cream
Glögg med nejlika grädde

Serves 6–8

5 gelatine leaves
750ml/1¼ pints/3 cups Swedish
   Glögg or mulled wine
15ml/1 tbsp caster (superfine) sugar

For the spiced cream

200ml/7fl oz/scant 1 cup double
   (heavy) cream
5ml/1 tsp icing (confectioner's) sugar
pinch of ground cloves

1 Soak the gelatine leaves in cold water until soft. Pour the Glögg wine into a pan and heat gently.

2 Stir the sugar into the wine until dissolved then add the softened gelatine leaves, which should melt in the hot wine. Pour the mixture into individual heatproof serving glasses, leave to cool, then place in the refrigerator for about an hour to set.

3 Whisk the cream until stiff then add the icing sugar and ground cloves. Just before serving, add a spoonful of the cream to each glass of jelly.

COOK'S TIP
Swedish Glögg is a mulled wine that is usually enjoyed at Christmas. It is served hot and has a robust alcohol content.

This delicious sweet was the result of a happy accident – some Glögg wine left over after a party and the inspired idea to make jelly with it.

Almond Pears
Mandelpäron

Serves 8

8 large ripe pears
juice of 1 lemon
25g/1oz/2 tbsp unsalted butter
350g/12oz/2 cups ground almonds
475ml/16fl oz/2 cups double (heavy)
    cream

This old-fashioned Swedish baked dessert is a tempting combination of cooked fruit and a sprinkling of ground almonds. The cream blends in with the juices and ground almonds to form a delicious sauce.

1 Preheat the oven to 180°C/350°F/Gas 4. Peel and halve the pears and remove the cores. Put the pears into an ovenproof dish and sprinkle with lemon juice to stop them going brown.

2 Put a small piece of butter on each pear and sprinkle the ground almonds evenly over the top. Bake in the oven for about 15 minutes, basting once or twice with the juice, until they begin to soften.

3 Meanwhile, whisk the cream until it is beginning to hold its shape. When the pears are cooked, pour over the whipped cream and serve immediately.

Swedish Apple Cake with Vanilla Cream
Appelkaka med vaniljkräm

Serves 6–8

115g/4½oz/½ cup plus 1 tbsp
  unsalted butter
7 eating apples
30ml/2 tbsp caster (superfine) sugar
10ml/2 tsp ground cinnamon
200g/7oz/1 cup sugar
2 egg yolks and 3 egg whites
100g/4oz/1 cup ground almonds
grated rind (zest) and juice of ½
  lemon

For the vanilla cream

250ml/8fl oz/1 cup milk
250ml/8fl oz/1 cup double (heavy)
  cream
15ml/1 tbsp sugar
1 vanilla pod (bean), split
4 egg yolks, beaten

1 Preheat the oven to 180°C/350°F/Gas 4. Butter a 20cm/8in flan tin (pan) using 15g/½oz/1 tbsp of the butter. Peel, core and thinly slice the apples and put the slices in a bowl. Add the caster sugar and cinnamon and mix them together. Put the mixture in the prepared tin.

2 Put the remaining butter and sugar in a bowl and whisk them together until they are light and fluffy. Beat in the egg yolks, then add the almonds and lemon rind and juice to the mixture.

3 Whisk the egg whites until stiff then fold into the mixture. Pour the mixture over the apples in the flan tin. Bake in the oven for about 40 minutes until golden brown and the apples are tender.

4 Meanwhile, make the vanilla cream. Put the milk, cream, sugar and vanilla pod in a pan and heat gently. Add a little of the warm milk mixture to the eggs then slowly add the egg mixture to the pan and continue to heat gently, stirring all the time, until the mixture thickens. Do not allow the mixture to boil or it will curdle.

5 Remove the vanilla pod and serve the vanilla cream warm or cold with the apple cake.

SERVING VARIATIONS

• Serve the apple cake with 300ml/½ pint/1¼ cups double (heavy) cream to which you have added 5ml/1 tsp vanilla sugar.

• Alternatively, serve with vanilla ice cream, which is particularly good if the cake is served warm.

Swedish apples are very sweet and ideally suited to this sublime cake. Apples form a significant part of Sweden's produce and survive the cold winters well. Kivik, a harbour town in Skåne in southern Sweden, is well known for its apple market and holds an annual festival where a huge picture is created, made entirely of apples.

Cloudberry Soufflé
Hjortron sufflé

1 Preheat the oven to 180°C/350°F/Gas 4. Grease an 18cm/7in soufflé dish with butter. Melt the butter in a pan, add the flour and cook over a low heat for 30 seconds, stirring to make a roux. Slowly add the milk, stirring continuously, to form a smooth sauce. Cook until the sauce boils and thickens.

2 Remove the sauce from the heat, leave to cool slightly then stir in the egg yolks. Add the cloudberry jam and cloudberry liqueur and turn into a large bowl.

3 In a large, separate bowl, whisk the egg whites until stiff then, using a metal spoon, fold them into the sauce. Put the mixture into the prepared soufflé dish and bake in the oven for about 20 minutes until risen. Serve the soufflé immediately.

Serves 6–8
50g/2oz/4 tbsp unsalted butter,
    plus extra for greasing
60ml/4 tbsp plain (all-purpose) flour
475ml/16fl oz/2 cups milk
4 egg yolks and 6 egg whites
275g/10oz/1 cup cloudberry jam
30ml/2 tbsp Lakka (Finnish
    cloudberry liqueur)

COOK'S TIPS
• The cloudberry jam could be replaced with another fruit jam.
• The cloudberry liqueur could be replaced with brandy or another fruit liqueur, such as crème de mûre or crème de framboise.

With cloudberries as the main ingredient, this dish is undeniably Scandinavian. Cloudberries are rare little golden raspberry-like berries with an exquisite taste that only grow wild in northern Scandinavia. Fresh ones are rarely available elsewhere, but the jam can be found in specialist stores.

Waffles with Spiced Blueberry Compote
Våflor med blåbärs kompott

Makes 20

25g/1oz/1 tbsp unsalted butter, plus
   extra for greasing
350g/12oz/3 cups plain (all-purpose)
   flour
350ml/12fl oz/1½ cups water
475ml/16fl oz/2 cups double (heavy)
   cream

For the spiced blueberry compote

200g/7oz blueberries, fresh or frozen
15ml/1 tbsp sugar
5ml/1 tsp balsamic vinegar
pinch of ground cinnamon
pinch of ground cloves

1 To make the spiced blueberry compote, put the blueberries into a pan, then add the sugar, vinegar, cinnamon and cloves and poach for about 5 minutes until soft and liquid. Bring to the boil and cook for a further 4 minutes to reduce the liquid. Either keep the compote warm, or cool and store in the refrigerator for up to 1 month.

2 To make the waffles, melt the butter. Put the flour in a large bowl and gradually beat in the water to form a smooth mixture then add the melted butter. Whisk the cream until stiff then fold into the mixture.

3 Preheat a waffle iron according to the manufacturer's instructions. Add a little butter to grease the waffle iron then place a dollop of waffle mixture in the iron. Cook the waffles until golden and crispy, keep warm and continue to cook the remaining waffle mixture, greasing the waffle iron each time with a little butter. Serve hot with the spiced blueberry compote.

VARIATION
Instead of the blueberry compote, serve the waffles with whipping cream and lingon conserve.

This recipe requires a waffle iron. If you have to purchase one it is unlikely that you will ever regret it, since waffles are so popular and are equally delicious with other stewed fruits or maple syrup. The blueberry compote can also be served with grilled goat's cheese, pancakes or rice pudding.

Makes 20

300ml/½ pint/1¼ cups milk
130g/4½oz/½ cup unsalted butter
a pinch of saffron threads
50g/2oz fresh yeast
700g/1½lb/6 cups plain (all-purpose) flour
5ml/1 tsp salt
150g/5oz/¾ cup caster (superfine) sugar
20 raisins
beaten egg, to glaze

Lucia Saffron Buns Lussekatter

1 Put the milk and butter in a pan and heat until the butter has melted. Remove from the heat, add the saffron threads and leave to cool until warm to the touch.

2 In a bowl, blend the fresh yeast with a little of the warm saffron milk. Add the remaining saffron milk then add the flour, salt and sugar. Mix together to form a dough that comes away from the sides of the bowl.

3 Turn the dough on to a lightly floured surface and knead for about 10 minutes until the dough feels firm and elastic. Shape into a ball, put in a clean bowl and cover with a clean dish towel. Leave to rise in a warm place for about 1 hour until the dough has doubled in size.

4 Turn the dough on to a lightly floured surface and knead again for 2–3 minutes. Divide the dough into 20 equal pieces. Form each piece into a roll, and then shape each roll into an S shape and place on greased baking sheets.

5 Place a raisin at the end of each bun. Cover with a clean dish towel and leave to rise in a warm place for about 40 minutes until doubled in size.

6 Preheat the oven to 200°C/400°F/Gas 6. Brush the tops of the buns with beaten egg to glaze and bake in the oven for about 15 minutes until golden brown.

On the 13th December, the Swedes celebrate the Italian festival of Saint Lucia to combat the effects of a long dark winter. These festival buns, flavoured with saffron, are made early in the morning of that day. They are called "lussekatter", or Lucia cats, because this is one of the shapes that are used for the buns.

Ginger Biscuits Pepparkakor

Makes about 50

150g/5½oz/10 tbsp butter
400g/14oz/2 cups sugar
50ml/2fl oz/¼ cup golden (light corn)
　syrup
15ml/1 tbsp treacle (molasses)
15ml/1 tbsp ground ginger
30ml/2 tbsp ground cinnamon
15ml/1 tbsp ground cloves
5ml/1 tsp ground cardamom
5ml/1 tsp bicarbonate of soda
　(baking soda)
240ml/8fl oz/1 cup water
150g/5oz/1¼ cups plain (all-
　purpose) flour

These biscuits are found all over Sweden. There is even a Swedish nursery rhyme saying that if you are very good you will be given Pepparkakor but if you are bad you will be given none!

1 Put the butter, sugar, syrup, treacle, ginger, cinnamon, cloves and cardamom in a heavy pan and heat gently until the butter has melted.

2 Put the bicarbonate of soda and water in a large heatproof bowl. Pour in the warm spice mixture and mix well together then add the flour and stir until well blended. Put in the refrigerator overnight to rest.

3 Preheat the oven to 220°C/425°F/Gas 7. Line several baking sheets with baking parchment. Knead the dough then roll out on a lightly floured surface as thinly as possible. Cut the dough into shapes of your choice and place on the baking sheets.

4 Bake the biscuits in the oven for about 5 minutes until golden brown, cooking in batches until all the biscuits are cooked. Leave to cool on the baking sheet.

Chocolate Gooey Cake Choklad kladd kaka

Serves 8

100g/4oz/½ cup unsalted butter,
    plus extra to grease
100g/4oz dark (bittersweet)
    chocolate with 75 per cent
    cocoa solids
5ml/1 tsp water
2 eggs, separated
175g/6oz/1½ cups ground almonds
5ml/1 tsp vanilla sugar
whipped double (heavy) cream,
    to serve

1 Preheat the oven to 180°C/350°F/Gas 4. Grease a 20cm/8in shallow round cake tin (pan) with a little butter. Break the chocolate into a pan. Add the water and heat gently until the chocolate has melted. Remove from the heat.

2 Cut the butter into small pieces, add to the chocolate and stir until melted. Add the egg yolks, ground almonds and vanilla sugar and stir together. Turn the mixture into a large bowl.

3 Whisk the egg whites until stiff then fold them into the chocolate mixture. Put the mixture into the prepared tin and bake in the oven for 15–17 minutes until just set. The mixture should still be soft in the centre. Leave to cool in the tin. When cold, serve with whipped cream.

This is Sweden's favourite chocolate cake. For perfect results it is essential to undercook the cake so that it is dense in the middle. Made with almonds instead of flour, Choklad Kladd Kaka is gluten free and therefore the perfect tempting, self-indulgent snack for a coeliac guest.

Crisp Rye Breads Knäckebröd

Makes 15

600ml/1 pint/2½ cups milk
50g/2oz fresh yeast
565g/1¼lb/5 cups rye flour plus
    225g/8oz/2 cups, for dusting
565g/1¼lb/5 cups strong white
    bread flour
10ml/2 tsp caraway or cumin seeds
5ml/1 tsp salt

1 Put the milk in a pan and heat gently until warm to the touch. Remove from the heat. In a bowl, blend the yeast with a little of the warmed milk. Add the remaining milk then add the rye flour, bread flour, caraway or cumin seeds and salt and mix together to form a dough.

2 Using the rye flour for dusting, turn the dough out on to a lightly floured surface and knead the dough for about 2 minutes. Cut the dough into 15 equal pieces then roll out each piece into a thin, flat round. Place on baking sheets and leave to rise in a warm place for 20 minutes.

3 Preheat the oven to 150°C/300°F/Gas 2. Using the rye flour, roll out the pieces of dough again into very thin, flat rounds. Return to the baking sheets. Make a pattern on the surface using a fork or knife.

4 Bake the breads in the oven for 8–10 minutes, turning after about 5 minutes, until hard and crispy. Transfer to a wire rack and leave to cool. Store the breads in an airtight container.

These traditional crispbreads were originally made with a hole in the centre so they could be hung over the oven to keep dry. Nowadays, they keep well in an airtight container. Knäckebröd is also sometimes made with rolled oats, in a similar way to sweet Scottish oatcakes.

Nutritional notes

Yellow Pea Soup: Energy 374kcal/1569kJ; Protein 25.8g; Carbohydrate 38.3g, of which sugars 3.7g; Fat 14g, of which saturates 4.3g; Cholesterol 33mg; Calcium 57mg; Fibre 3.9g; Sodium 988mg.

Nettle Soup with Egg Butterballs: Energy 239kcal/982kJ; Protein 2g; Carbohydrate 1.5g, of which sugars 1.3g; Fat 24.5g, of which saturates 14.8g; Cholesterol 109mg; Calcium 68mg; Fibre 0.7g; Sodium 141mg.

Lacy Potato Pancakes: Energy 182kcal/767kJ; Protein 3.9g; Carbohydrate 33.1g, of which sugars 3.3g; Fat 4.6g, of which saturates 1.8g; Cholesterol 5mg; Calcium 20mg; Fibre 2.7g; Sodium 38mg.

Toast Skagen: Energy 415kcal/1726kJ; Protein 14.5g; Carbohydrate 15.2g, of which sugars 2.5g; Fat 33.4g, of which saturates 9.2g; Cholesterol 180mg; Calcium 128mg; Fibre 0.7g; Sodium 1065mg.

Gralax with Mustard and Dill Sauce: Energy 543kcal/2258kJ; Protein 26.4g; Carbohydrate 21g, of which sugars 20.7g; Fat 39.8g, of which saturates 5.4g; Cholesterol 63mg; Calcium 58mg; Fibre 0.3g; Sodium 428mg.

Stuffed Cabbage Rolls: Energy 169kcal/702kJ; Protein 9.2g; Carbohydrate 16.1g, of which sugars 5.2g; Fat 7.6g, of which saturates 3.3g; Cholesterol 47mg; Calcium 49mg; Fibre 1.8g; Sodium 51mg.

Jansson's Temptation: Energy 400kcal/1669kJ; Protein 9.4g; Carbohydrate 36.5g, of which sugars 6.1g; Fat 25.1g, of which saturates 14.6g; Cholesterol 69mg; Calcium 115mg; Fibre 2.5g; Sodium 696mg.

Poached Turbot with Egg and Prawns: Energy 350kcal/1448kJ; Protein 20.8g; Carbohydrate 0.8g, of which sugars 0.7g; Fat 29.2g, of which saturates 17.1g; Cholesterol 113mg; Calcium 71mg; Fibre 0.5g; Sodium 337mg.

Fried Mackerel with Rhubarb Chutney: Energy 353kcal/1470kJ; Protein 19.9g; Carbohydrate 16.7g, of which sugars 9.1g; Fat 23.4g, of which saturates 5.9g; Cholesterol 63mg; Calcium 54mg; Fibre 0.7g; Sodium 90mg.

Lax Pudding: Per portion Energy 137kcal/573kJ; Protein 9.9g; Carbohydrate 7.2g, of which sugars 2.4g; Fat 7.8g, of which saturates 3.9g; Cholesterol 70mg; Calcium 59mg; Fibre 0.8g; Sodium 525mg.

Salted Salmon with Potatoes in Dill Sauce: Energy 407kcal/1699kJ; Protein 26.4g; Carbohydrate 22.6g, of which sugars 5.9g; Fat 24g, of which saturates 9.7g; Cholesterol 85mg; Calcium 155mg; Fibre 1g; Sodium 118mg.

Stuffed Guinea Fowl with Wild Mushrooms: Energy 348kcal/1462kJ; Protein 27.7g; Carbohydrate 26g, of which sugars 2.4g; Fat 15.6g, of which saturates 3.6g; Cholesterol 77mg; Calcium 49mg; Fibre 1.8g; Sodium 226mg.

Gotland Lamb Burgers Stuffed with Blue Cheese: Energy 345kcal/1433kJ; Protein 18g; Carbohydrate 7g, of which sugars 1.2g; Fat 27.2g, of which saturates 16.5g; Cholesterol 116mg; Calcium 116mg; Fibre 0.5g; Sodium 310mg.

Sailor's Steak: Energy 279kcal/1170kJ; Protein 19.4g; Carbohydrate 29.9g, of which sugars 9.7g; Fat 6.6g, of which saturates 3.2g; Cholesterol 50mg; Calcium 38mg; Fibre 2.3g; Sodium 70mg.

Prune-stuffed Loin of Pork with Hasselback Potatoes: Energy 538kcal/2247kJ; Protein 16.7g; Carbohydrate 42.8g, of which sugars 15.1g; Fat 34.6g, of which saturates 18.5g; Cholesterol 95mg; Calcium 46mg; Fibre 4g; Sodium 248mg.

Swedish Hash: Energy 930kcal/3866kJ; Protein 55.9g; Carbohydrate 18.7g, of which sugars 3.6g; Fat 70.9g, of which saturates 28.8g; Cholesterol 427mg; Calcium 68mg; Fibre 1.3g; Sodium 1992mg.

Baked Sausage Terrine with Lingonberry Conserve: Energy 238kcal/1003kJ; Protein 15.6g; Carbohydrate 28.5g, of which sugars 17.8g; Fat 7.7g, of which saturates 3.1g; Cholesterol 91mg; Calcium 134mg; Fibre 1.5g; Sodium 105mg.

Reindeer Stroganoff: Energy 486kcal/2019kJ; Protein 30.2g; Carbohydrate 7.8g, of which sugars 5.1g; Fat 38.2g, of which saturates 22g; Cholesterol 148mg; Calcium 57mg; Fibre 0.9g; Sodium 274mg.

Elk Meatballs with Lingon: Energy 1655kcal/6860kJ; Protein 79.6g; Carbohydrate 40.7g, of which sugars 13.2g; Fat 129.2g, of which saturates 64.8g; Cholesterol 552mg; Calcium 205mg; Fibre 3.2g; Sodium 666mg.

Carpaccio of Cured Venison: Energy 153kcal/651kJ; Protein 27.8g; Carbohydrate 6.5g, of which sugars 6.5g; Fat 2.8g, of which saturates 1g; Cholesterol 63mg; Calcium 10mg; Fibre 0g; Sodium 69mg.

Glögg Jelly with Clove Cream: Energy 1577kcal/6524kJ; Protein 4g; Carbohydrate 24.8g, of which sugars 24.8g; Fat 107.4g, of which saturates 66.8g; Cholesterol 274mg; Calcium 161mg; Fibre 0g; Sodium 98mg.

Almond Pears: Energy 607kcal/2511kJ; Protein 10.5g; Carbohydrate 15.3g, of which sugars 14.1g; Fat 56.4g, of which saturates 21.8g; Cholesterol 81mg; Calcium 147mg; Fibre 5.7g; Sodium 23mg.

Swedish Apple Cake with Vanilla Cream: Energy 541kcal/2254kJ; Protein 7.6g; Carbohydrate 39.7g, of which sugars 39.3g; Fat 40.3g, of which saturates 20g; Cholesterol 227mg; Calcium 122mg; Fibre 2.1g; Sodium 135mg.

Cloudberry Soufflé: Energy 284kcal/1198kJ; Protein 6.7g; Carbohydrate 44.9g, of which sugars 37.4g; Fat 9g, of which saturates 4.7g; Cholesterol 118mg; Calcium 102mg; Fibre 0.2g; Sodium 129mg.

Waffles with Spiced Blueberry Compote: Energy 189kcal/787kJ; Protein 2.12g; Carbohydrate 14.52g, of which sugars 1.18g; Fat 14.03g, of which saturates 8.62g; Cholesterol 35mg; Calcium 41mg; Fibre 0,85g; Sodium 14mg.

Lucia Saffron Buns: Energy 423kcal/1788kJ; Protein 9.2g; Carbohydrate 81.7g, of which sugars 15.1g; Fat 8.8g, of which saturates 5g; Cholesterol 20mg; Calcium 161mg; Fibre 2.8g; Sodium 69mg.

Ginger Biscuits: Energy 31kcal/130kJ; Protein 0.2g; Carbohydrate 5.8g, of which sugars 4.2g; Fat 0.8g, of which saturates 0.5g; Cholesterol 2mg; Calcium 5mg; Fibre 0.1g; Sodium13mg.

Chocolate Gooey Cake: Energy 311kcal/1288kJ; Protein 6.8g; Carbohydrate 10g, of which sugars 9.3g; Fat 27.4g, of which saturates 9.9g; Cholesterol 75mg; Calcium 66.2mg; Fibre 1.9g; Sodium 97mg.

Crisp Rye Breads: Energy 323kcal/1376kJ; Protein 9.2g; Carbohydrate 71.1g, of which sugars 2.4g; Fat 2.2g, of which saturates 0.7g; Cholesterol 2mg; Calcium 118mg; Fibre 7.3g; Sodium 19mg.

Index